Scientists in Action

by D. Michael Kim
Illustrated by Bruce Day

Editorial Offices: Glenview, Illinois • Parsippany, New Jersey • New York, New York
Sales Offices: Needham, Massachusetts • Duluth, Georgia • Glenview, Illinois
Coppell, Texas • Sacramento, California • Mesa, Arizona

You probably know the word *science*—the study of nature and the physical world. And you probably know the word *scientists*—people who study nature and the physical world.

But did you know this? All over the world, scientists learn about nature and the physical world in very similar ways. They use scientific methods.

---

physical world: things we can see, feel, and touch

A medieval Persian doctor treating a patient

A Persian doctor named Al-Razi may have been the first person to use what we call scientific methods. Al-Razi was born around the year 864 and died around 930. Building on Greek ideas, he used scientific methods to choose the best place to build a hospital in Baghdad, Iraq.

The Scientific Method

Scientists use scientific methods to find answers to questions. Here is one way to describe the steps that scientists follow.

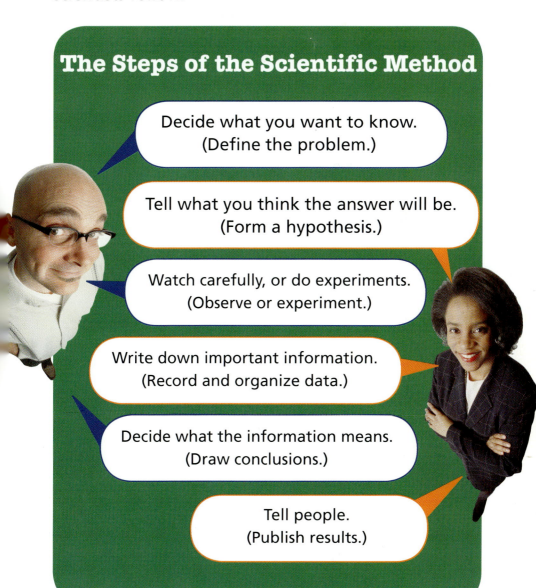

The Steps of the Scientific Method

- Decide what you want to know. (Define the problem.)
- Tell what you think the answer will be. (Form a hypothesis.)
- Watch carefully, or do experiments. (Observe or experiment.)
- Write down important information. (Record and organize data.)
- Decide what the information means. (Draw conclusions.)
- Tell people. (Publish results.)

Let's take a look at how these steps worked in a real experiment—a famous one by Benjamin Franklin.

Define the Problem

Benjamin Franklin began experimenting with electricity in 1747. Ben was an inventor, and he loved thunderstorms! They made him think. Both lightning and electricity send out sparks of light. Both make crackling noises. "Can lightning and electricity be the same thing?" he wondered.

In the 1700s, many houses were made of wood. Sometimes lightning struck them, and they burned. Ben thought, "Maybe there is a way to protect people and buildings from lightning."

Ben defined the problem: "Lightning causes damage, so how can I protect people and buildings from fires?"

Form a Hypothesis

Ben knew that iron attracts electricity. His earlier experiments proved that. So Ben asked more questions. "If lightning is electricity, will iron attract lightning too? What if I put an iron pole, or rod, on top of a building? What will happen?"

Ben formed two hypotheses:
- Lightning is electricity.
- An iron rod on top of a building will attract lightning to it, so the lightning will hit the rod instead of the building.

---

iron: a strong metal

Thirteen American Colonies Along the Coast of the Atlantic Ocean

Before there was a United States, there were thirteen American colonies along the coast of the Atlantic Ocean. The colonies were ruled by England, so the people living there were subjects of the British king. Ben Franklin was very important in the colonies. He was an inventor, a writer, and a printer of books. He even helped the colonies become free of British rule.

The thirteen colonies

Experiment

First, Ben had to prove that lightning is electricity. "If it is," he thought, "and if iron can attract lightning, then a lightning rod made of iron might protect buildings and people." So, on a rainy night in 1752, Ben did an experiment.

Ben and his son, William, made a kite out of two strips of wood and a piece of cloth. They tied a wire to one of the wooden strips and tied a key to the other end of the wire. Ben tied a string to the key and held onto the string. Electricity can't travel along a string, so the string would protect Ben. At least that's what he hoped!

Ben let the kite fly up into the storm. As the kite flew high in the sky, lightning struck the wire! Electricity traveled down the wire to the key. He touched the key with his finger, and a spark flew out! Ouch! A shock!

Draw Conclusions

Ben had proved one hypothesis: Lightning is electricity. Now he had to prove the other: that a tall, iron rod can protect a building from lightning. Ben would need to prove this through observation or experiments. Still, he was on his way to inventing the lightning rod. Eventually, he did it.

Record and Organize Data

Ben skipped a step that most scientists take. Oh, Ben! You should have recorded and organized your data! Fifteen years later, someone else wrote down what had happened in Ben's experiment.

And one more thing, Ben. That experiment was really dangerous! You could have been killed! People who tried to repeat your experiment have been killed by lightning. Readers, don't ever try it!

Publish Results

Ben told people about the lightning rod. It took a while for people to believe that an iron rod could protect buildings from fires. Then they argued about whether it should be pointed or have a flat, blunt end. Ben thought it should be pointed. The king of England liked blunt ones.

Many colonists thought the king was a scoundrel. So within a few years, pointed lightning rods protected homes and buildings all over the colonies.

Ben had done it. He had invented the lightning rod, and he used a scientific method to do it. Way to go, Ben!

Talk About It

1. Do you think the author wrote this book to entertain readers or to explain ideas? What makes you think so?
2. What steps did Ben follow in his experiment?

Write About It

3. Make a chart on a separate sheet of paper. Write the steps of scientific methods. Give examples of each step. You may use Ben's experiment or an experiment of your own.

Step	Example
Define the problem.	
Form a hypothesis.	

Extend Language

A person who studies science is called a *scientist*. What word describes the methods that scientists use and also begins with *scient–*?

Photography Credits: 2 ©Historical Picture Archives/CORBIS; 3 (L) ©Getty Creative/RF, (R) ©Getty Creative/RF.

ISBN: 0-328-14227-1

Copyright © Pearson Education, Inc.

All Rights Reserved. Printed in the United States of America.

This publication is protected by Copyright, and permission should be obtained from the publisher prior to any prohibited reproduction, storage in a retrieval system, or transmission in any form by any means, electronic, mechanical, photocopying, recording, or likewise. For information regarding permission(s), write to: Permissions Department, Scott Foresman, 1900 East Lake Avenue, Glenview, Illinois 60025.

3 4 5 6 7 8 9 10 V0G1 14 13 12 11 10 09 08 07

ELL Reader

Science

Genre	Build Background	Access Content	Extend Language
Nonfiction	• Inventors and Inventions • Scientific Methods • American Colonies	• Graphic Aids • Historical Notes • Labels • Map • Definitions	• Words Related to *science*

Scott Foresman Reading Street 5.3.1

scottforesman.com

ISBN 0-328-14227-1

9 780328 142279